SCHIRMER'S LIBRARY
OF MUSICAL CLASSICS

Vol. 2057

JOHANN SEBASTIAN BACH

The Well-Tempered Clavier
48 Preludes and Fugues

COMPLETE
Books I and II

For Piano

Edited and fingered by Carl Czerny

ISBN: 978-0-634-09921-2

T0055319

G. SCHIRMER, *Inc.*

DISTRIBUTED BY

HAL•LEONARD®
CORPORATION
7777 W. BLUEMOUND RD. P.O. BOX 13819 MILWAUKEE, WI 53213

Johann Sebastian Bach
(1685–1750)

Johann Sebastian Bach was a towering figure in Baroque music. Along with his contemporary George Frideric Handel, Bach defined the sounds of his era, creating a timeless body of remarkable musical literature. His genius as a composer was not widely recognized during his lifetime, and it was not until the mid-19th century that Bach's music began to be heard widely in Europe.

Born into a family with seven generations of musicians on March 21, 1685, Bach spent his early years in the German town of Eisenach. He studied at the Latin School where his cousin served as organist. This proved to make a profound impression on the young boy. By 1695, young Sebastian and his brother Jacob were orphaned and sent to live with their older brother Johann Christoph in Ohrdruf. There, Bach studied organ and received a classical education at the Lyceum school. He began to teach himself music by hand-copying Johann Christoph's scores. In 1700, when Christoph's home was becoming cramped, Sebastian headed for Lüneburg in northern Germany, where his musical education continued with singing (until his voice broke), and performing as an organist. Sebastian's love for the organ, both playing and building, was nurtured here with directed musical studies and exposure to important organists from the north German tradition.

In 1703 Bach received his first official post as a musician at Arnstadt, where he played organ for services, and composed music. As a young man, Bach's curiosity to hear and learn from various composers and performers often spurred him to make lengthy visits to other cities, though he was nearly penniless. He walked 30 to 60 miles from Arnstadt to other cities to hear great organists of his day, including Dietrich Buxtehude. The post at Arnstadt was not without its difficulties. Sebastian's intolerance for less able musicians at the local church resulted in scuffles, and his exalted musical demands and long absences tried his employers.

Bach landed a better position as organist for the church of St. Blasius in Mühlhausen in 1707. While there he began composing cantatas and teaching pupils. Shortly thereafter, he and his wife, Maria Barbara, moved to Weimar. Sebastian was appointed as Duke Wilhelm's court organist and eventually Konzertmeister. He met and befriended the composer George Philipp Telemann, who later became godfather to one of Bach's sons. In Weimar, Bach composed the six *English Suites*. His reputation as a harpsichordist, organist and supervisor for organ building grew, with his name first appearing in print when Johann Mattheson referred to him as the "famous Weimar organist." In 1717 he traveled to Dresden and was invited to compete at the harpsichord with the French virtuoso Louis Marchand, who apparently fled from the competition.

Relations eventually soured between Sebastian and the duke, and when Prince Leopold of Cöthen offered the composer a better paying position as Kapellmeister, Bach left Weimar. The prince was a learned music lover who furnished Bach with living quarters, good musicians, and various instruments. Bach's stay at Cöthen from 1717 to 1723 was a fertile period for instrumental compositions, which included the six Brandenburg concertos, six cello suites, two orchestral suites, the *Clavier Büchlein* (Little Clavier Notebook), and the beginnings of his *Orgelbüchlein* (Little Organ Book) and *Das wohltemperirte Clavier* (The Well-Tempered Clavier).

In July of 1720 Bach returned home from a trip with the prince to Carlsbad and discovered that his wife had died. In December of 1721 he married Anna Magdalena, a singer who became an integral part of Bach's musical life. She assisted her husband as a performer and copyist, and took to the task of raising a burgeoning family household.

In 1722 the prestigious post of Kantor at the Thomaskirche in Leipzig became available, when the noted German composer Joseph Kuhnau died. The vacancy at Leipzig solicited many strong candidates, including Telemann. The list of applicants shrank due to their inability or unwillingness to teach Latin. Bach was not the ecclesiastic council's first choice, but he was offered the position and settled in Leipzig in May of 1723. He would remain in the city for the rest of his life. His responsibilities included working as the director of music at Leipzig's four main churches, serving as Cantor at the St. Thomas school, and directing music for civic occasions.

Bach had at his disposal in Leipzig many students and musicians to help fill the musical needs of the various churches. He was in continual demand as a supervisor for new organs being built in the area, and he was also consulted by the piano maker Gottfried Silbermann. He poured his energies into the composition of about 300 sacred cantatas for weekly services, and composed many other important sacred works in Leipzig, including the *St. Matthew Passion* (1727), the *Christmas Oratorio* (1734), several motets, and the monumental *Mass in B minor* (1749). Bach continued to write instrumental music, including harpsichord concertos and a large collection of keyboard works published in installments entitled *Clavier Übung*. The collection included the six partitas and the *Italian Concerto* for keyboard, chorale preludes for organ, and the *Goldberg Variations*. This latter work was presented to Count von Keyserlingk in Dresden. According to legend the count had his harpsichordist, Johann Gottlieb Goldberg, play the variations to alleviate his insomnia.

Bach's most auspicious occasion may have been his visit to the court of Frederick the Great, King of Prussia, in 1747. He gave concerts for the court, including a fugal improvisation on a theme supplied to him by the king. Upon returning home, Bach worked diligently on *Musikalishes Opfer* (Musical Offering) which contained the improvised fugue along with several other movements for keyboard, flute and violin and continuo, all based on the king's theme.

One of Bach's last works was *Die Kunst der Fuge* (The Art of Fugue). As Bach worked toward its completion, he became blind, and his health weakened. He died at home on July 28, 1750, leaving behind an estate overflowing with musical instruments and manuscripts. Carl Phillip Emanuel Bach saw to the completed publication of *Die Kunst der Fuge*.

The Well-Tempered Clavier

Bach was a staunch believer in a thorough musical education for his Leipzig students and his own children. The family possessed many instruments, and many keyboard pieces were written specifically for Bach's sons. (Emanuel and Johann Christian eventually became the most successful heirs to his compositional craft.) Sebastian's creative impulses were often guided by a sense of pedagogical purpose. The 48 preludes and fugues of *The Well-Tempered Clavier* are an encyclopedic demonstration of the various styles of the Baroque period. While Bach's fame did not reach beyond Germany until the mid-19th century, study of his works was essential to the musical development of composers such as Beethoven and Chopin. Bach's exhaustive treatment and development of the fugue, along with his inventive rhythmic and harmonic language, inspired countless composers after him.

One reason Bach composed *The Well-Tempered Clavier* was to advocate the use of well-tempered tuning. While not the first musical work written to encompass all 24 keys, it was (and is) the most influential and celebrated. Temperament refers to a slight alteration of an acoustically pure interval. If a keyboard instrument is tuned based on pure perfect fifths (known as Pythagorean tuning), certain enharmonic pitches (G-sharp and A-flat, for example) will differ in pitch by nearly an eighth of a tone. Well-tempering refers to any tuning method in which all major and minor keys sound satisfactorily in tune by slightly modifying certain pure intervals. The 12 half-step intervals comprising an octave are not necessarily exactly equal in a well-tempered tuning, but that is the aural illusion. This tuning allowed all keys to be treated equally.

The traditional, prevailing tuning method in Bach's time was mean-tone temperament. It was widely used beginning in the 16th century, and its use continued into the early years of the 19th century. The object of this tuning was to slightly modify pure perfect fifths to preserve pure major thirds, within a particular range of the tonic. This method was more "in tune" than well-tempered tuning in keys that were no more than three fifths sharp or two fifths flat of the tonic. For example, if the instrument was tuned with C as the tonic, the other usable keys in the tuning would be G, D, A, F, and B-flat. However, if a piece modulated outside of that range, the instrument would sound badly out of tune. As music became more tonally complex and chromatic, mean-tone temperament fell out of practice. This musical trend led eventually to equal temperament (a form of well-tempered tuning) becoming the standard modern piano tuning. Equal temperament is a form of well-temperament in which the 12 half-step intervals comprising an octave are exactly equal.

Contents

Book I

BOOK II

The Well-Tempered Clavier

Book I

PRELUDE NO. 1

in C major

Johann Sebastian Bach

All figures in the fingering which are set a-
bove the notes are intended, whether in inner
or outer parts, for the right hand; whereas, the
figures below the notes are for the left hand.
This explanation will suffice to show, in doubt-
ful cases, by which hand any note in the inner
parts is to be played.

Alle Fingersatz-Zahlen, welche über den Noten
stehen, gelten (auch in den Mittelstimmen) stets der
rechten Hand. Dagegen sind die unter den Noten
stehenden Zahlen immer für die linke Hand bestimmt.
Dieses reicht hin, um in zweifelhaften Fällen an-
zuzeigen, von welcher Hand jede Note in den Mittelstimmen gegriffen werden muss.

FUGUE NO. 1
in C major

Johann Sebastian Bach

PRELUDE NO. 2

in C minor

Johann Sebastian Bach

Allegro vivace. (♩ = 144.)

FUGUE NO. 2
in C minor

Johann Sebastian Bach

PRELUDE NO. 3
in C-sharp major

Johann Sebastian Bach

FUGUE NO. 3

in C-sharp major

Johann Sebastian Bach

PRELUDE NO. 4

in C-sharp minor

Andante con moto. (♩ = 92)

Johann Sebastian Bach

FUGUE NO. 4
in C-sharp minor

Johann Sebastian Bach

PRELUDE NO. 5

in D major

Johann Sebastian Bach

FUGUE NO. 5

in D major

Johann Sebastian Bach

PRELUDE NO. 6
in D minor

Allegro moderato. (♩ = 80)

Johann Sebastian Bach

FUGUE NO. 6

in D minor

Johann Sebastian Bach

PRELUDE NO. 7
in E-flat major

Johann Sebastian Bach

FUGUE NO. 7

in E-flat major

Johann Sebastian Bach

PRELUDE NO. 8
in E-flat minor

Johann Sebastian Bach

FUGUE NO. 8
in E-flat minor

Johann Sebastian Bach

PRELUDE NO. 9

in E major

Johann Sebastian Bach

FUGUE NO. 9

in E major

Johann Sebastian Bach

PRELUDE NO. 10
in E minor

Allegro molto moderato. (♩=84.)

Johann Sebastian Bach

FUGUE NO. 10
in E minor

Johann Sebastian Bach

PRELUDE NO. 11

in F major

Johann Sebastian Bach

FUGUE NO. 11

in F major

Johann Sebastian Bach

PRELUDE NO. 12

in F minor

Andante espressivo. (♪= 104.)

Johann Sebastian Bach

FUGUE NO. 12
in F minor

Johann Sebastian Bach

PRELUDE NO. 13

in F-sharp major

Johann Sebastian Bach

FUGUE NO. 13

in F-sharp major

Johann Sebastian Bach

Allegretto piacevole. ($\quad$ = 88.)

PRELUDE NO. 14

in F-sharp minor

Johann Sebastian Bach

FUGUE NO. 14

in F-sharp minor

Johann Sebastian Bach

PRELUDE NO. 15
in G major

Johann Sebastian Bach

FUGUE NO. 15
in G major

Johann Sebastian Bach

Allegretto vivace. (♩.=80.)

PRELUDE NO. 16

in G minor

Johann Sebastian Bach

FUGUE NO. 16

in G minor

Johann Sebastian Bach

PRELUDE NO. 17

in A-flat major

Johann Sebastian Bach

FUGUE NO. 17

in A-flat major

Johann Sebastian Bach

PRELUDE NO. 18

in G-sharp minor

Johann Sebastian Bach

Allegretto moderato ed espressivo. (♩ = 126.)

FUGUE NO. 18
in G-sharp minor

Johann Sebastian Bach

PRELUDE NO. 19

in A major

Johann Sebastian Bach

FUGUE NO. 19

Allegro moderato. (♩.= 69.)

PRELUDE NO. 20

in A minor

Johann Sebastian Bach

FUGUE NO. 20

in A minor

Johann Sebastian Bach

PRELUDE NO. 21

in B-flat major

Johann Sebastian Bach

FUGUE NO. 21

in B-flat major

Johann Sebastian Bach

PRELUDE NO. 22

in B-flat minor

Johann Sebastian Bach

FUGUE NO. 22
in B-flat minor

Johann Sebastian Bach

PRELUDE NO. 23

in B major

Johann Sebastian Bach

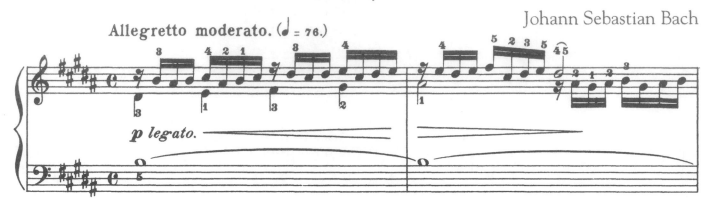

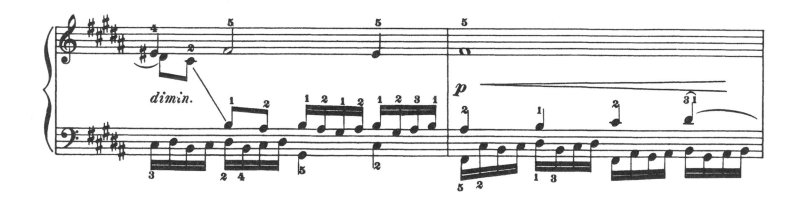

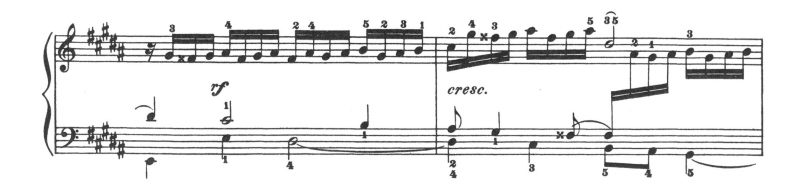

FUGUE NO. 23

in B major

Johann Sebastian Bach

PRELUDE NO. 24

in B minor

Johann Sebastian Bach

FUGUE NO. 24

in B minor

Johann Sebastian Bach

The Well-Tempered Clavier

Book II

PRELUDE NO. 1

in C major

Johann Sebastian Bach

FUGUE NO. 1
in C major

Johann Sebastian Bach

PRELUDE NO. 2
in C minor

Johann Sebastian Bach

FUGUE NO. 2

in C minor

Johann Sebastian Bach

Moderato quasi Andante. (♩ = 69.)

PRELUDE NO. 3

in C-sharp major

Johann Sebastian Bach

FUGUE NO. 3

in C-sharp major

Johann Sebastian Bach

PRELUDE NO. 4

in C-sharp minor

Johann Sebastian Bach

FUGUE NO. 4

in C-sharp minor

Johann Sebastian Bach

Allegro vivace. (♩.=72.)

143

PRELUDE NO. 5

in D major

Johann Sebastian Bach

FUGUE NO. 5

in D major

Johann Sebastian Bach

PRELUDE NO. 6
in D minor

Johann Sebastian Bach

Allegro vivace. (♩ = 126.)

FUGUE NO. 6

in D minor

Johann Sebastian Bach

PRELUDE NO. 7

in E-flat major

Johann Sebastian Bach

FUGUE NO. 7

in E-flat major

Johann Sebastian Bach

Allegro maestoso. (♩ = 132.)

PRELUDE NO. 8

in D-sharp minor

Johann Sebastian Bach

FUGUE NO. 8
in D-sharp minor

Johann Sebastian Bach

Andante serioso ed espressivo. ($\quarternote$=56.)

PRELUDE NO. 9
in E major

Johann Sebastian Bach

Lento moderato. (♩ = 80.)

FUGUE NO. 9
in E major

Johann Sebastian Bach

Adagio alla Breve. (♩ = 60.)

p legatissimo e pesante.

PRELUDE NO. 10

in E minor

Johann Sebastian Bach

Allegretto vivace. (♩.= 66.)
p
cresc.
f
p
cresc.
f
p
cresc.
f
sf
dim.

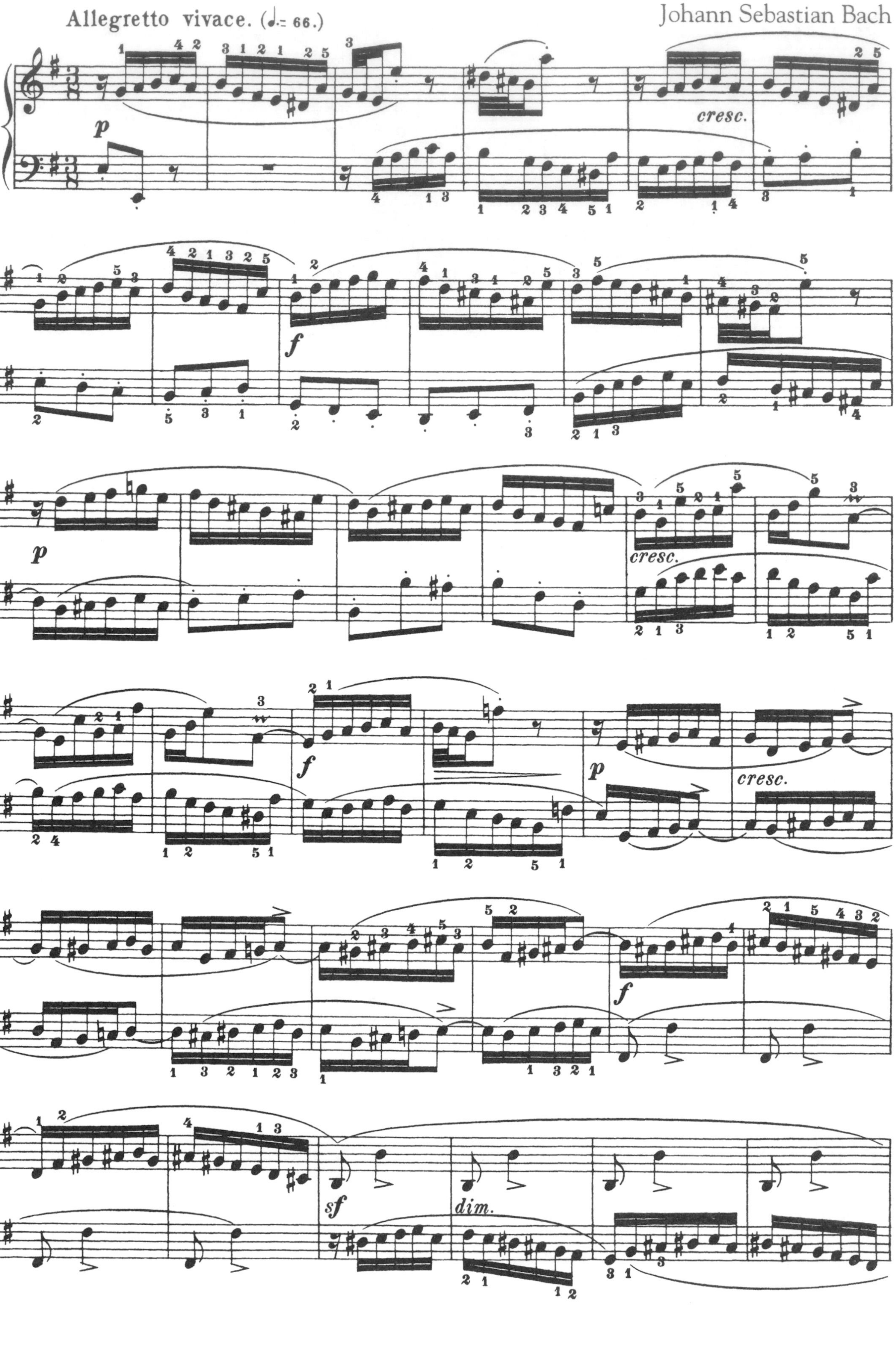

FUGUE NO. 10

in E minor

Johann Sebastian Bach

*1) The 16th-note and the last of the three 8th-notes are to be played exactly together.

*2) The same here, and everywhere throughout the Fugue, where this division of the beat appears.

PRELUDE NO. 11
in F major

Johann Sebastian Bach

FUGUE NO. 11

in F major

Johann Sebastian Bach

PRELUDE NO. 12

in F minor

Johann Sebastian Bach

FUGUE NO. 12

in F minor

Johann Sebastian Bach

PRELUDE NO. 13

in F-sharp major

Johann Sebastian Bach

FUGUE NO. 13

in F-sharp major

Johann Sebastian Bach

PRELUDE NO. 14

in F-sharp minor

Johann Sebastian Bach

Andante con moto. (♪ = 116)

FUGUE NO. 14

in F-sharp minor

Johann Sebastian Bach

Allegro moderato e spiritoso. (♩ = 108)

PRELUDE NO. 15
in G major

Johann Sebastian Bach

Allegro vivace. (♩ = 132.)

FUGUE NO. 15

in G major

Johann Sebastian Bach

PRELUDE NO. 16
in G minor

Johann Sebastian Bach

FUGUE NO. 16
in G minor

Johann Sebastian Bach

Andante con moto. (♩ = 84.)

PRELUDE NO. 17

in A-flat major

Johann Sebastian Bach

FUGUE NO. 17
in A-flat major

Johann Sebastian Bach

PRELUDE NO. 18
in G-sharp minor

Johann Sebastian Bach

Allegro moderato. (♩ = 100.)

FUGUE NO. 18

in G-sharp minor

Johann Sebastian Bach

Moderato e quieto. ($\bullet$ = 56.)

PRELUDE NO. 19

in A major

Johann Sebastian Bach

Allegretto vivace. (♩.= 88.)

FUGUE NO. 19

in A major

Johann Sebastian Bach

Allegro moderato. (♩ = 96.)

PRELUDE NO. 20

in A minor

Johann Sebastian Bach

FUGUE NO. 20
in A minor

Johann Sebastian Bach

Andante maestosso ed energico. ($\quarternote = 66.$)

PRELUDE NO. 21

in B-flat major

Johann Sebastian Bach

FUGUE NO. 21

in B-flat major

Johann Sebastian Bach

PRELUDE NO. 22

in B-flat minor

Johann Sebastian Bach

FUGUE NO. 22

in B-flat minor

Johann Sebastian Bach

PRELUDE NO. 23

in B major

Johann Sebastian Bach

FUGUE NO. 23

in B major

Johann Sebastian Bach

PRELUDE NO. 24

in B minor

Johann Sebastian Bach

Allegro. (♩ = 80.)

FUGUE NO. 24
in B minor

Johann Sebastian Bach